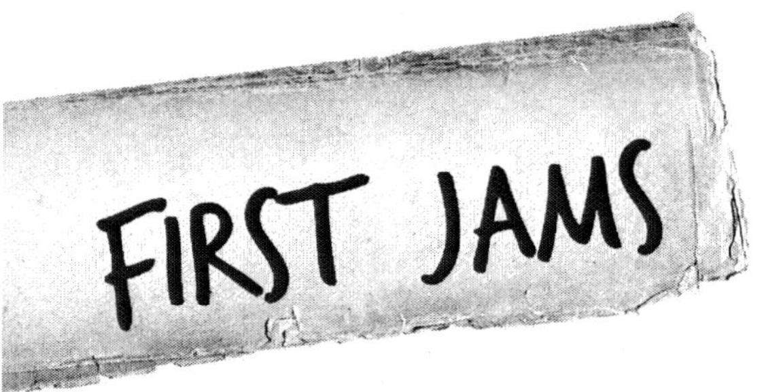

UKULELE

BY LEE "DREW" ANDREWS

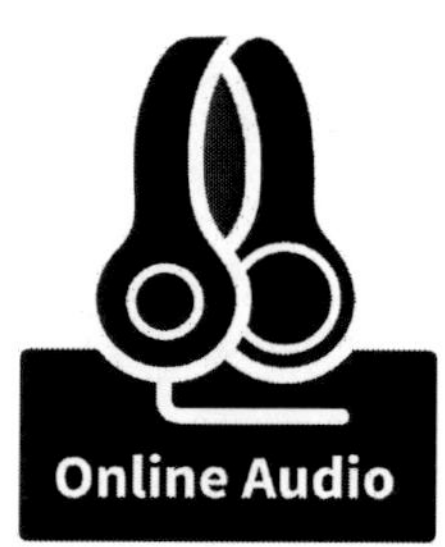

www.melbay.com/21512BCDEB

Audio Contents

1 Aura Lee
2 Aura Lee Backup
3 Blackberry Blossom
4 Blackberry Blossom Backup
5 Careless Love
6 Careless Love Backup
7 Cindy
8 Cindy Backup
9 Cripple Creek
10 Cripple Creek Backup
11 Cumberland Gap
12 Cumberland Gap Backup
13 Hand Me Down My Walking Cane
14 Hand Me Down My Walking Cane Backup
15 Irish Washerwoman
16 Irish Washerwoman Backup
17 Lil' Liza Jane
18 Lil' Liza Jane Backup
19 Man of Constant Sorrow
20 Man of Constant Sorrow Backup
21 Oh, Sinner Man
22 Oh, Sinner Man Backup
23 Old Dan Tucker
24 Old Dan Tucker Backup
25 Old Joe Clark
26 Old Joe Clark Backup
27 Planxty Irwin
28 Planxty Irwin Backup
29 Roll In My Sweet Baby's Arms
30 Roll In My Sweet Baby's Arms Backup
31 Shady Grove
32 Shady Grove Backup
33 Sourwood Mountain
34 Sourwood Mountain Backup
35 The Wabash Cannonball
36 The Wabash Cannonball Backup
37 Wildwood Flower
38 Wildwood Flower Backup
39 Will The Circle Be Unbroken
40 Will The Circle Be Unbroken Backup

Cover instrument: Lanikai LFM-S Soprano Ukulele
www.lanikaiukes.com

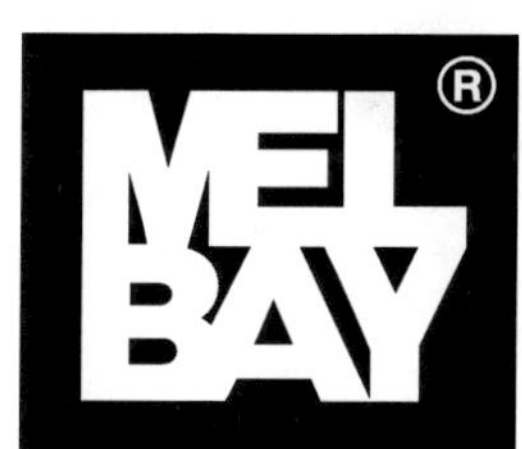

Visit us on the Web at www.melbay.com — E-mail us at email@melbay.com

Introduction

The First Jam series was created to give beginners of all ages a book of simple, common tunes to learn. Many are standard "Jam" tunes in the Bluegrass/Old Time music styles. All the books in this series are written in the same key; they can all be played together without any problems. So get your friends or family who play guitar, mandolin, banjo, ukulele, dulcimer or Dobro together, grab these books and start jamming.

Improvisation – Another idea behind writing the First Jam series was to provide a number of tunes that were easy to learn, but that are also great to begin working on improvising. Each book offers the melody for that particular instrument as well as back-up chords for another instrument to accompany you. Have fun!

Songs

Aura Lee 3
Blackberry Blossom 4
Careless Love 5
Cindy 6
Cripple Creek 7
Cumberland Gap 8
Hand Me Down My Walking Cane 9
Irish Washerwoman 10
Lil' Liza Jane 11
Man of Constant Sorrow 12
Oh, Sinner Man 13
Old Dan Tucker 14
Old Joe Clark 15
Planxty Irwin 16
Roll in My Sweet Baby's Arms 18
Shady Groove 19
Sourwood Mountain 20
The Wabash Cannonball 21
Wildwood Flower 22
Will The Circle Be Unbroken 23

Thanks for all your help and support (in no specific order): Tim Godwin at Line6, Mark Wilson at OnBoard Research, David Lienhard at Dean Markley Strings, Mario Biferali at Godin Guitars, Chaz Winzenread at Michael Kelly Guitars, Rick Gagliano, and Gary Davis. My wife, children and parents for all their support and understanding.

Aura Lee

1 Melody

2 Backup

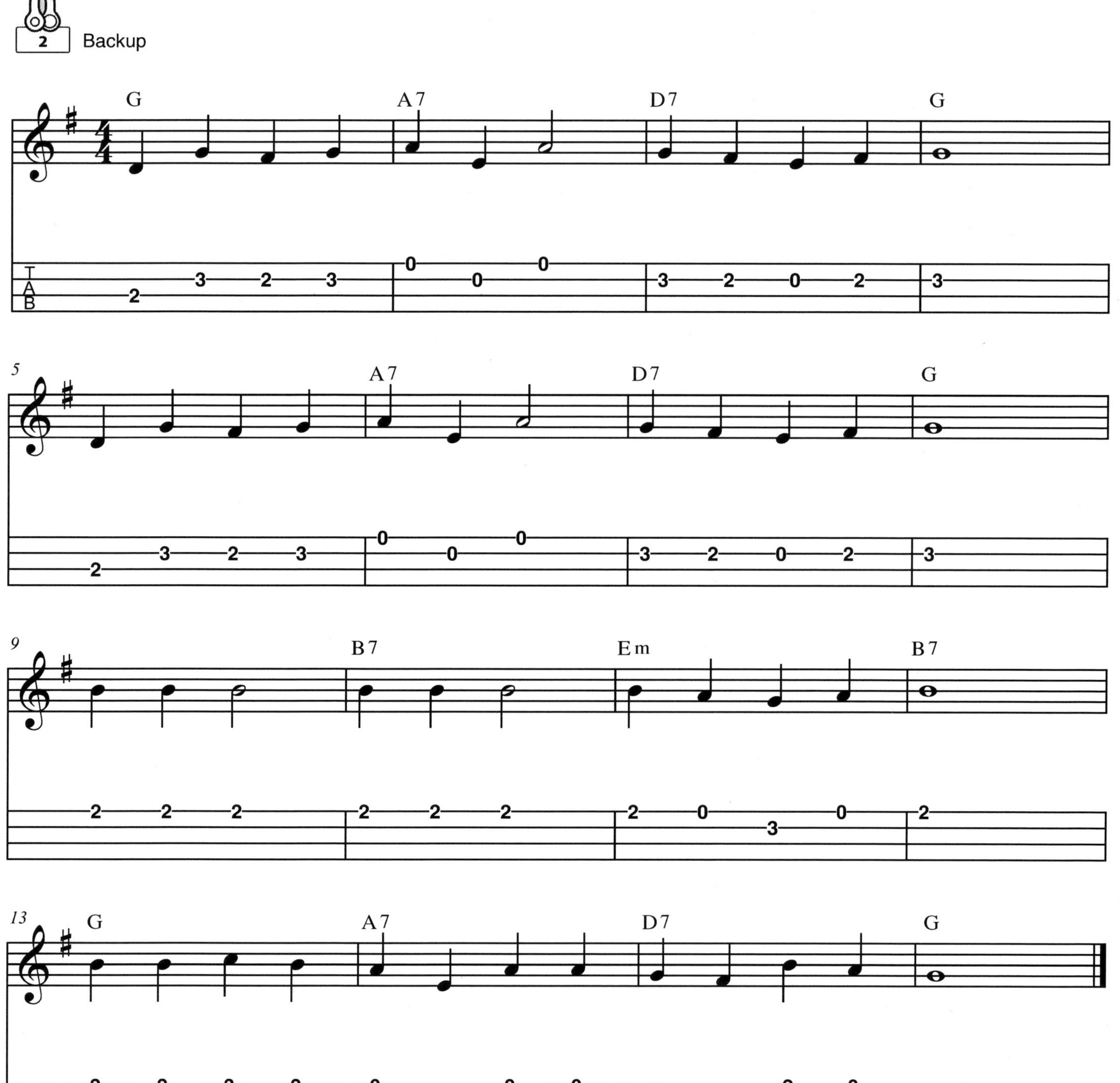

Blackberry Blossom

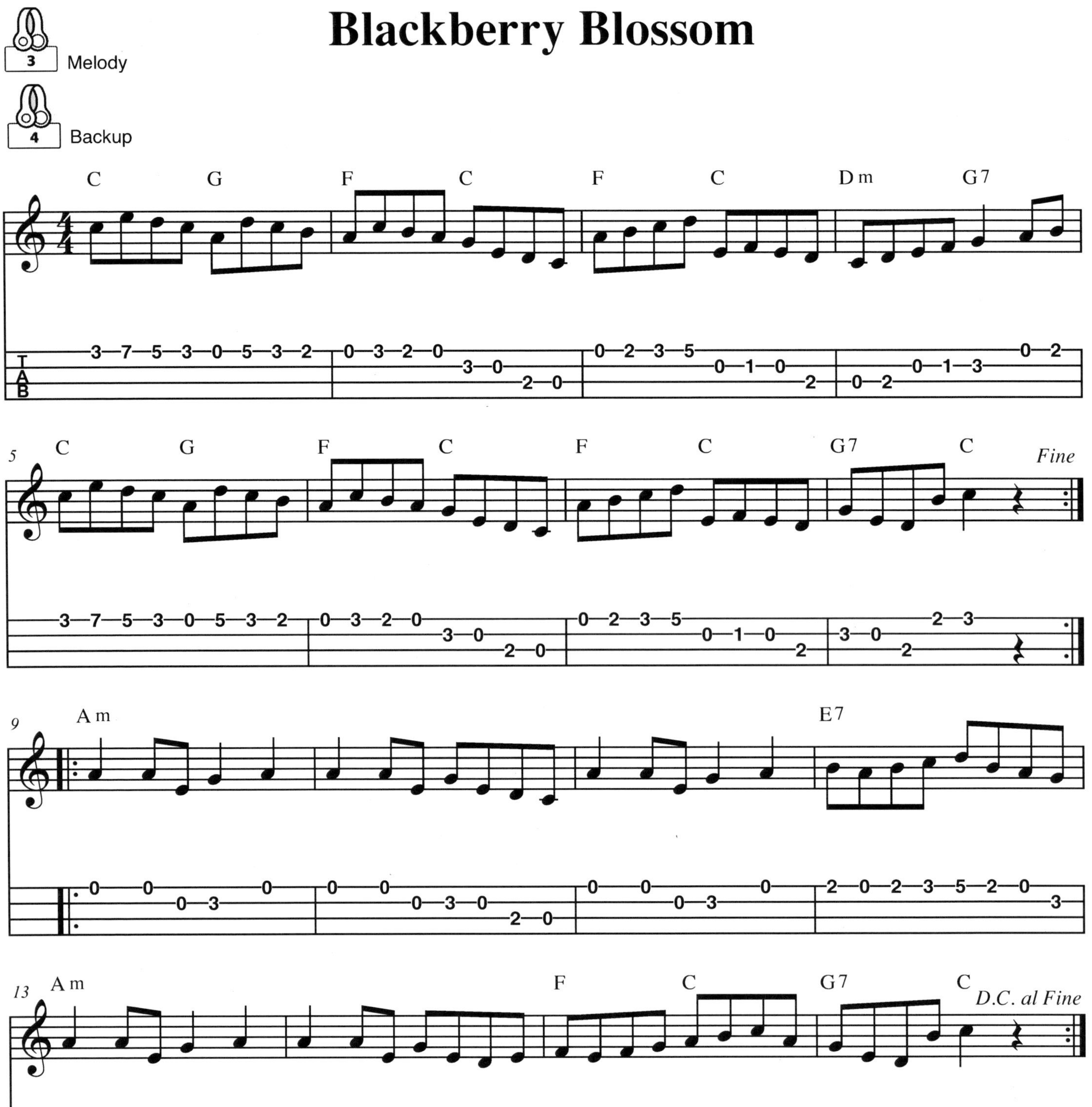

Careless Love

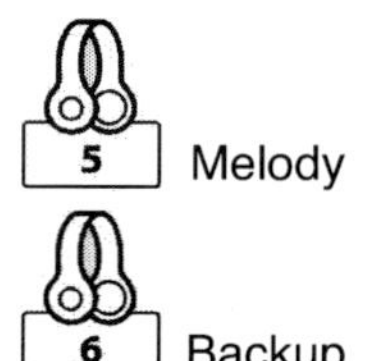

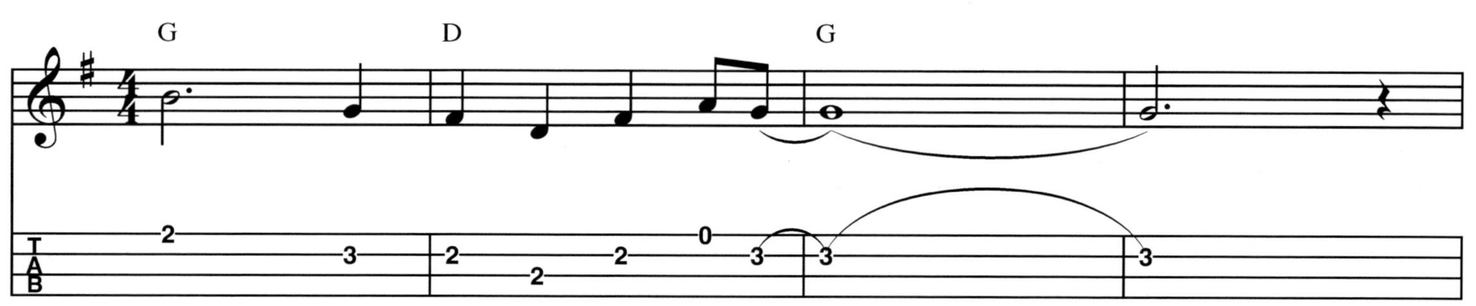

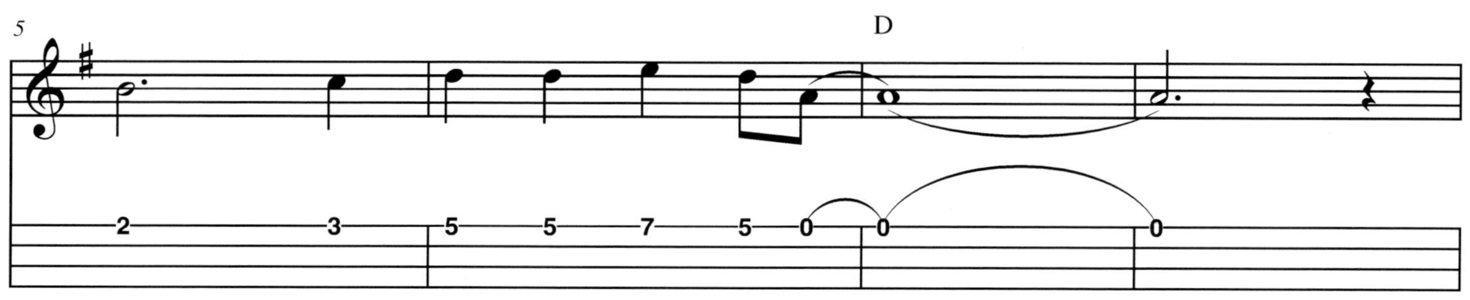

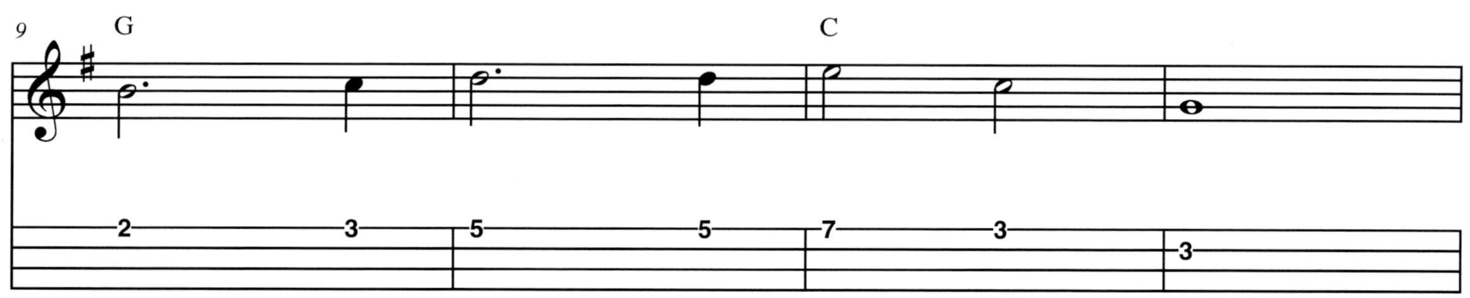

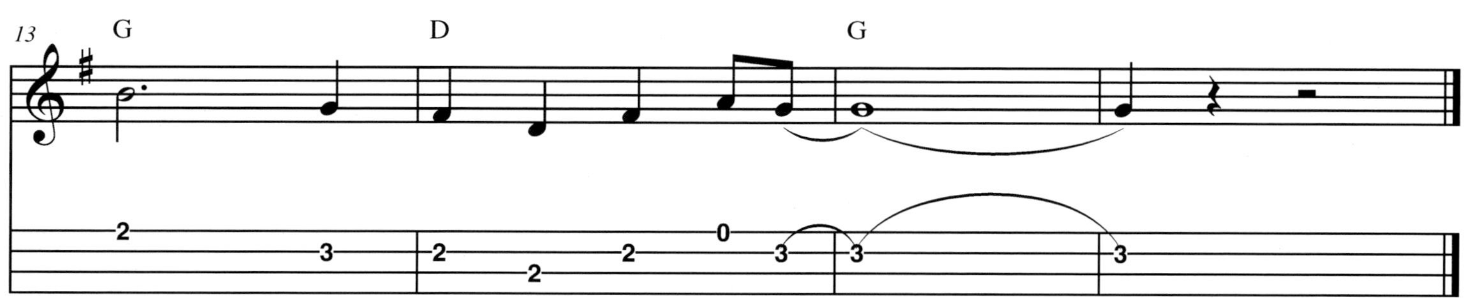

Cindy

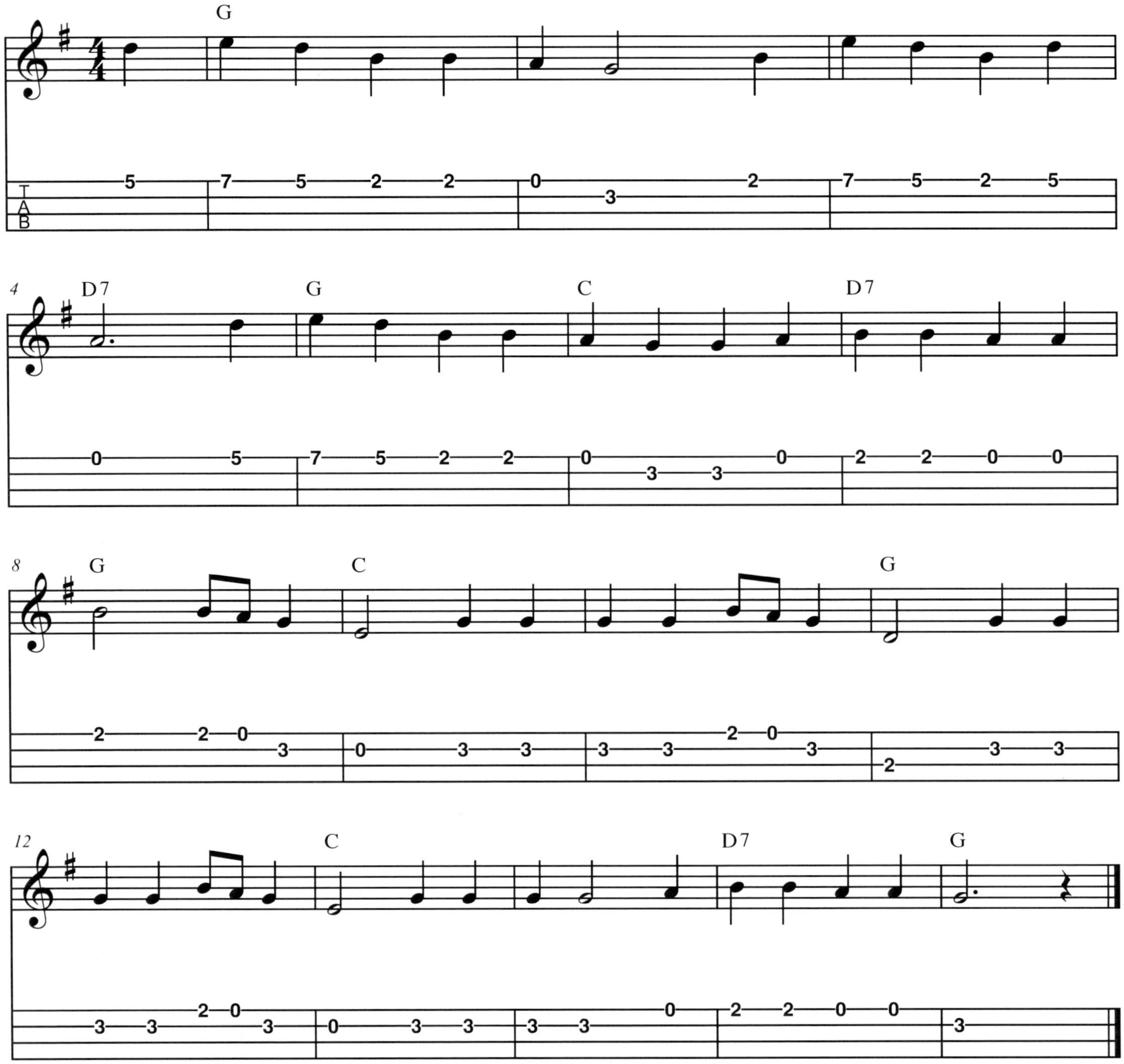

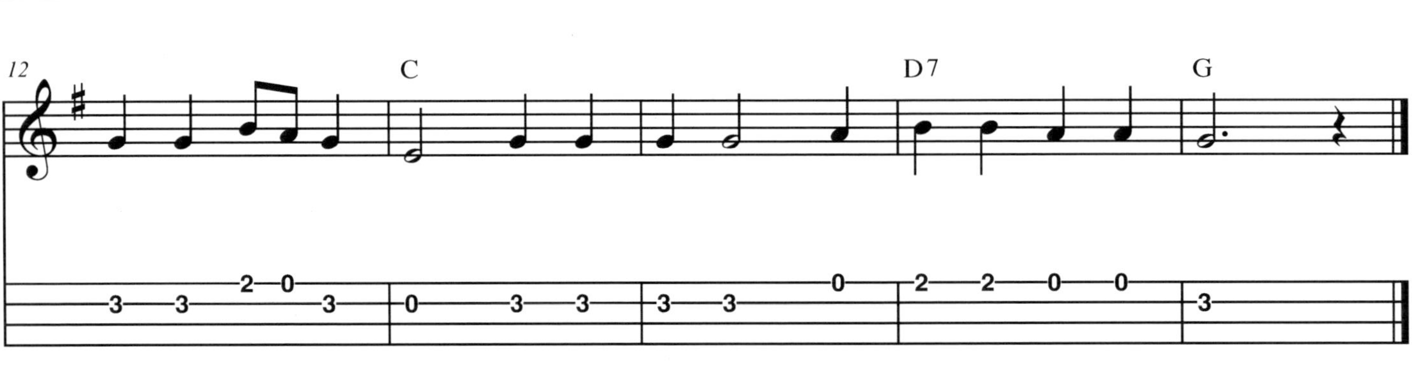

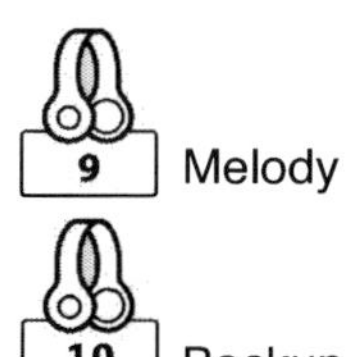

Cripple Creek

D G D A7 D

T
A
B

5
D G D A7 D

9
D G D D G E7 A7

13
D G D G A7 D

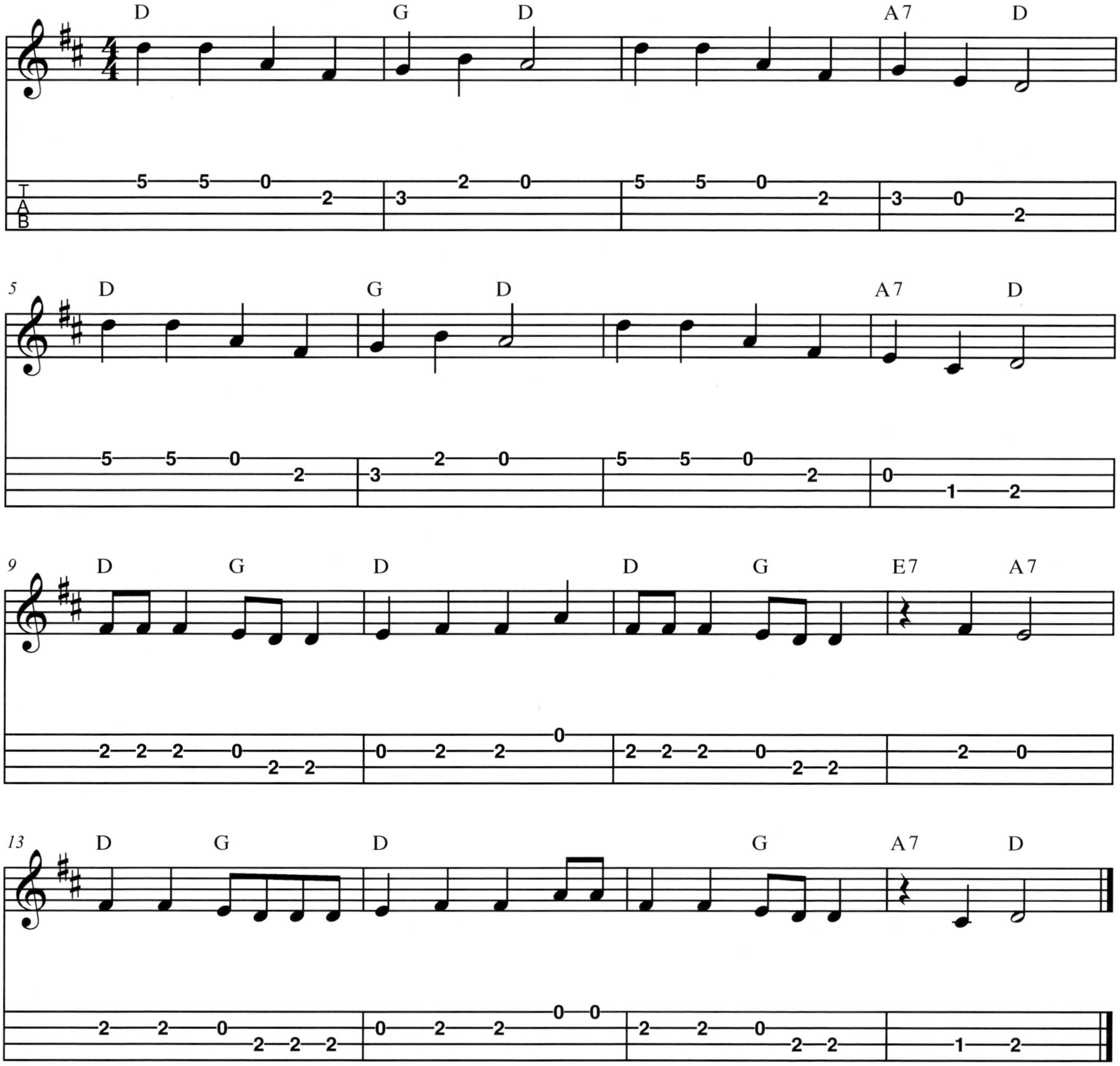

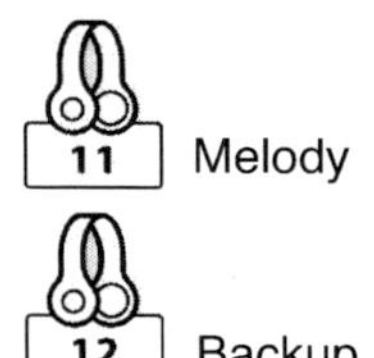

Cumberland Gap

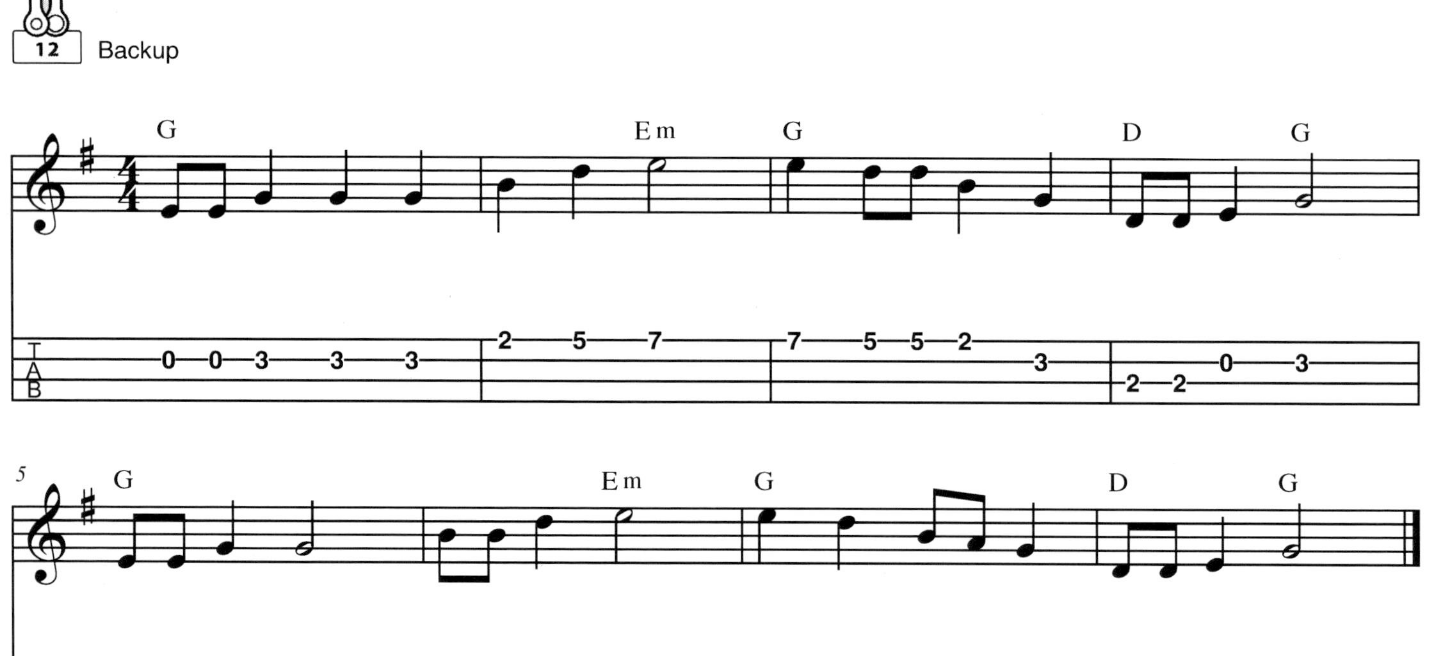

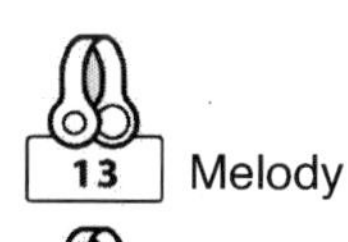

Melody

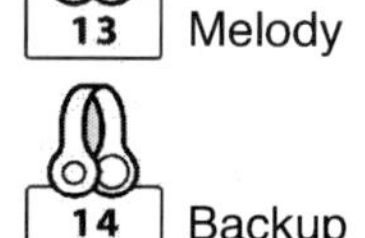

Backup

Hand Me Down My Walking Cane

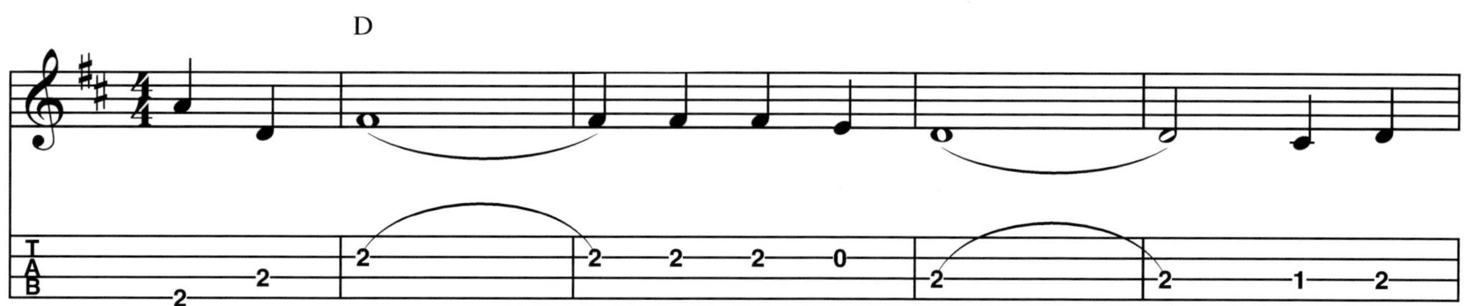

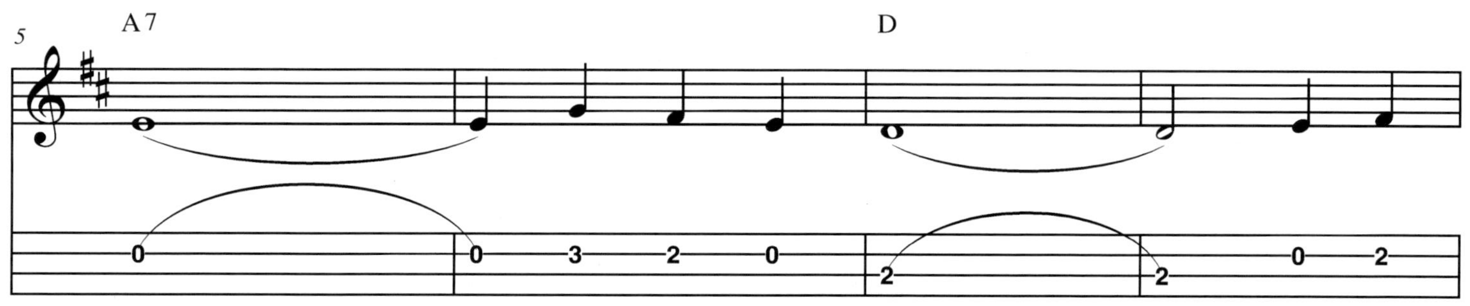

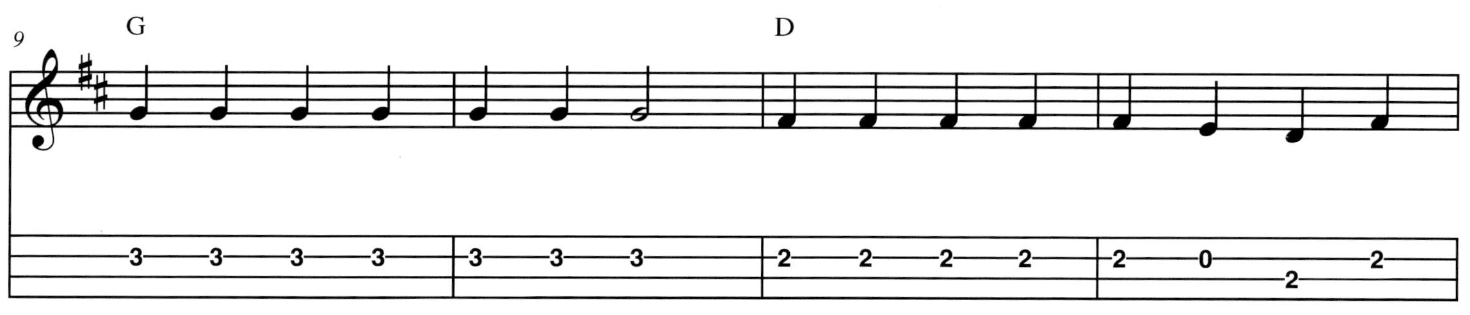

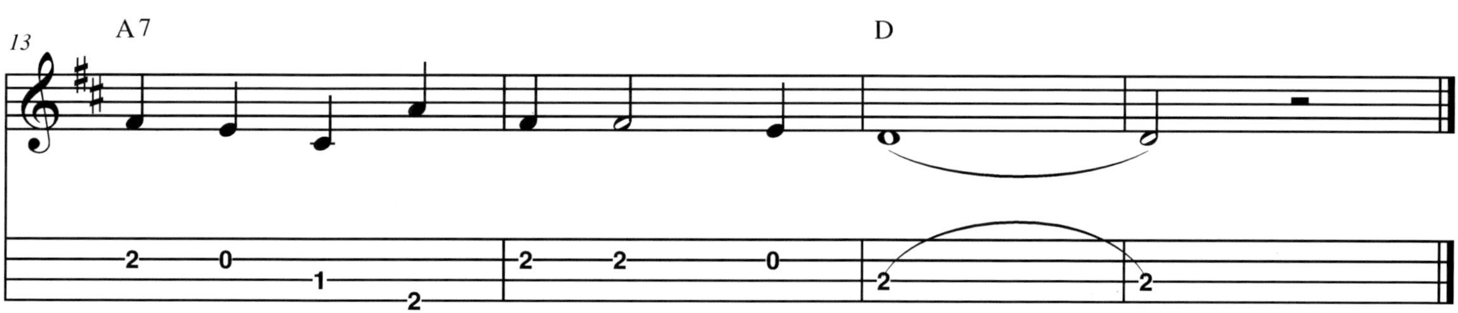

Irish Washerwoman

15 Melody

16 Backup

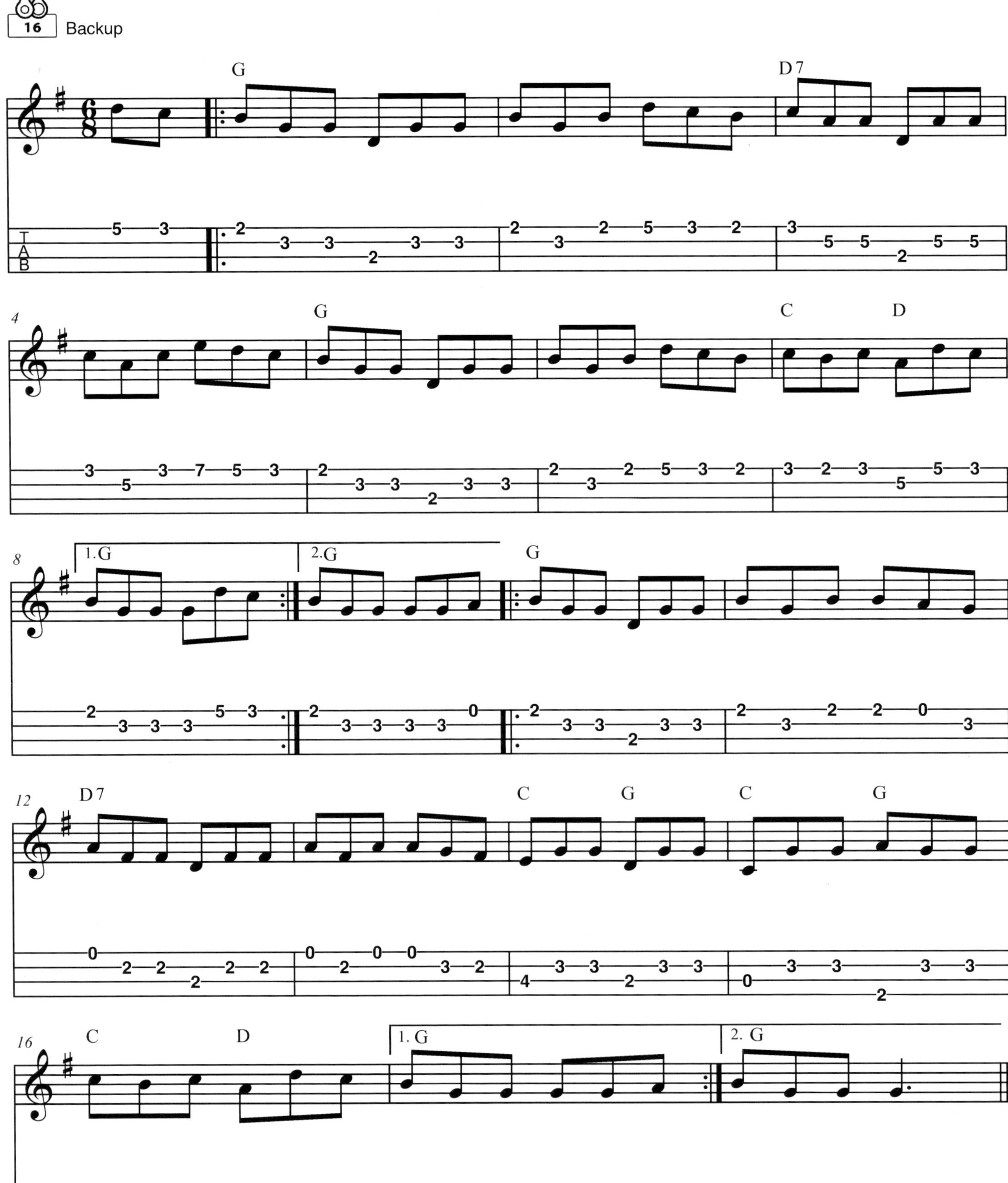

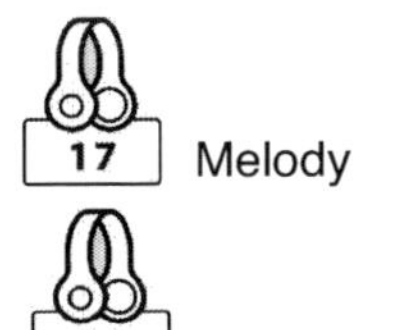

Lil' Liza Jane

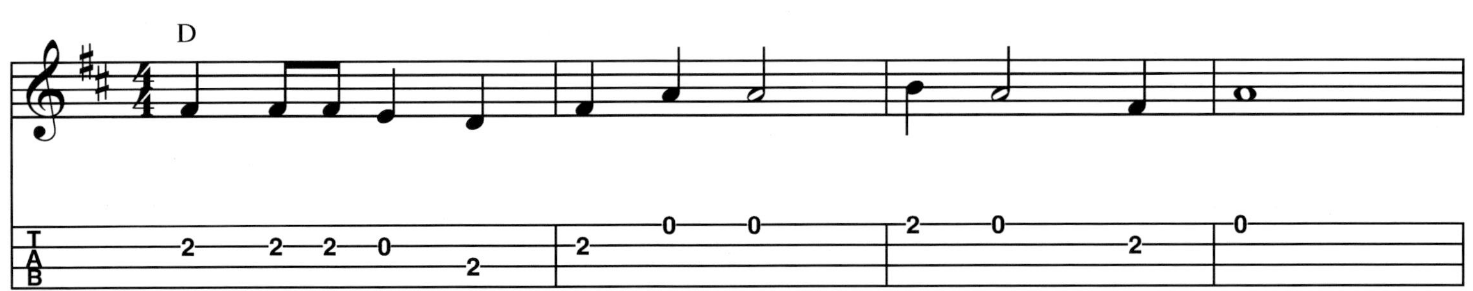

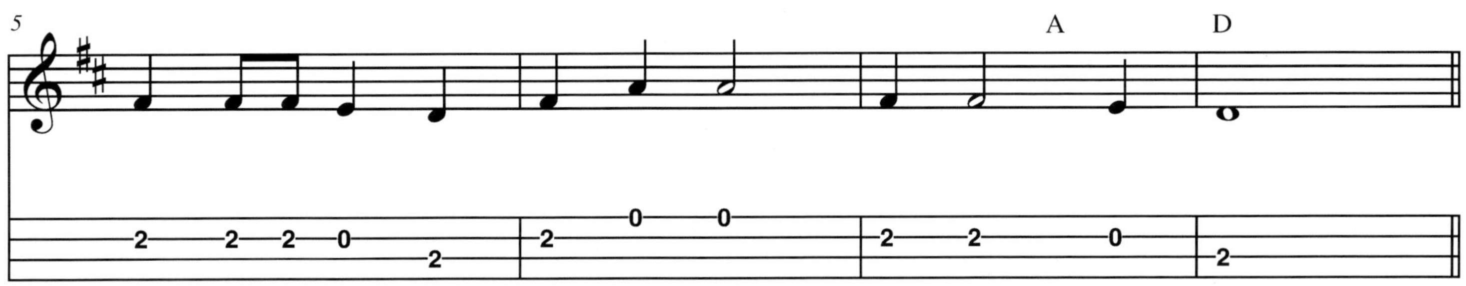

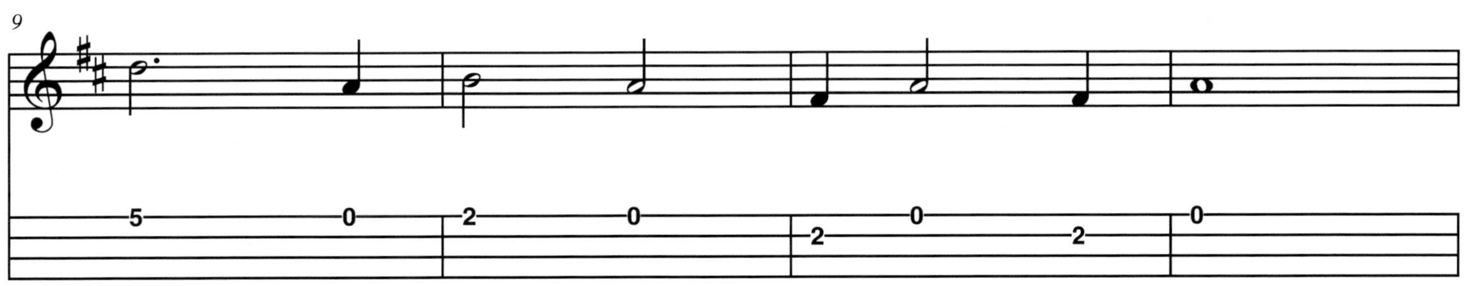

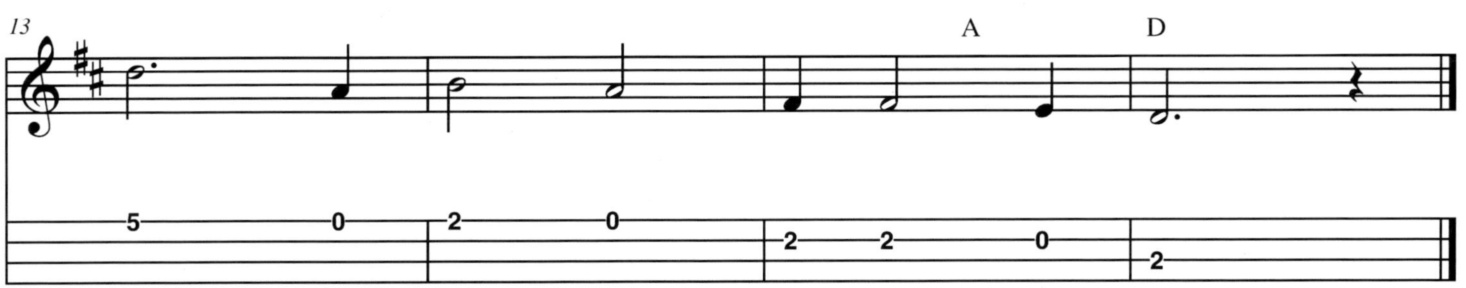

Man of Constant Sorrow

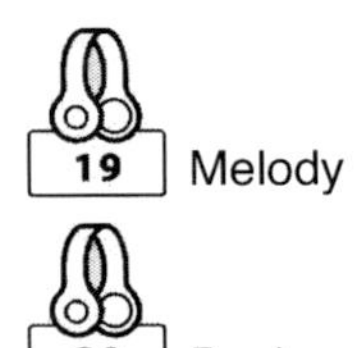

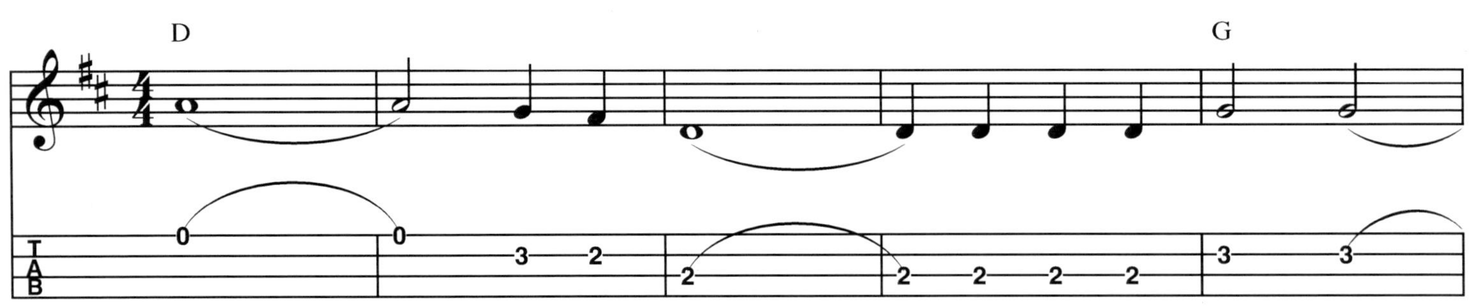

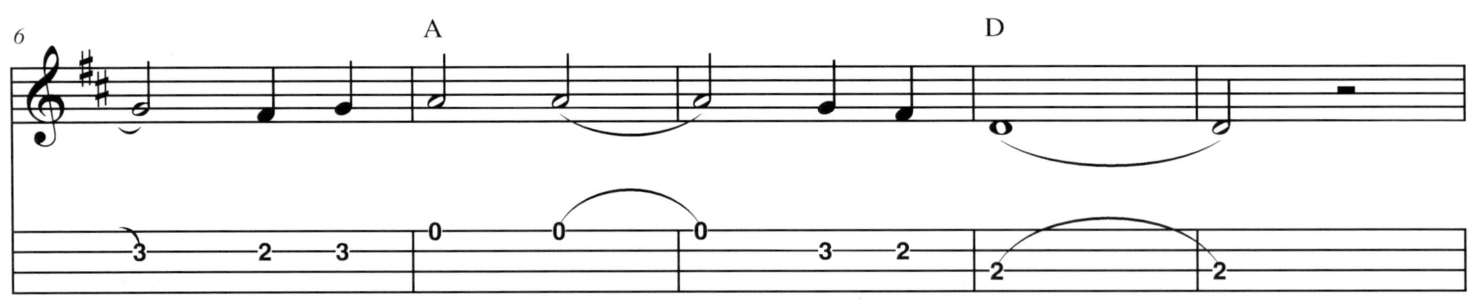

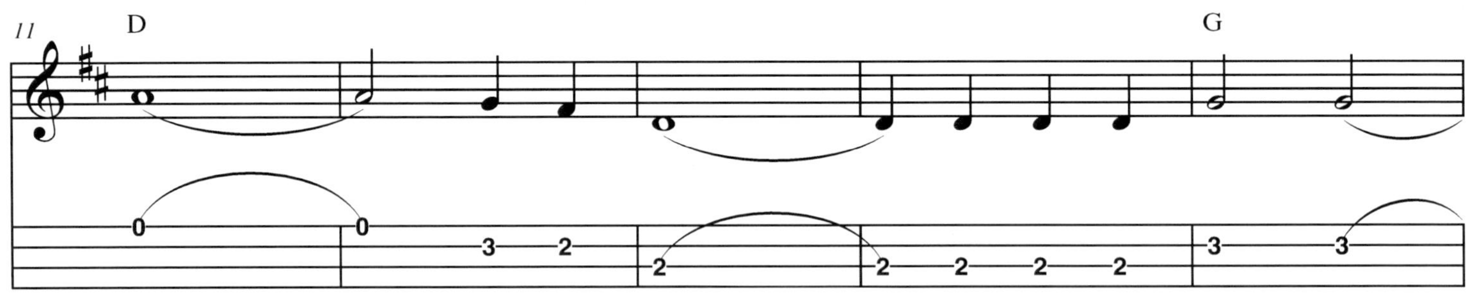

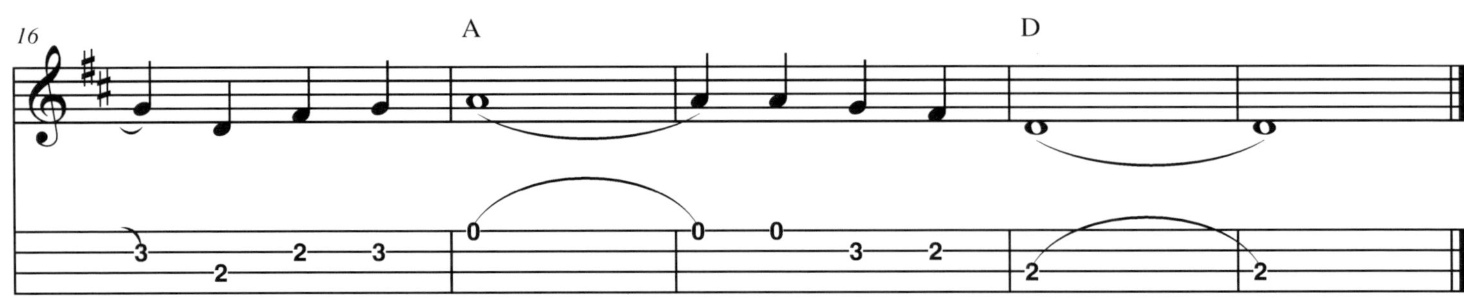

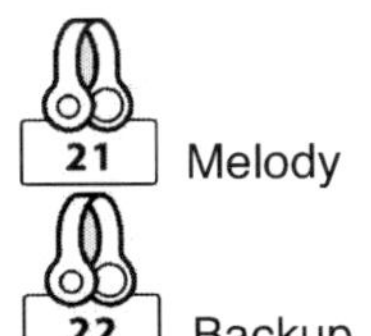

Oh, Sinner Man

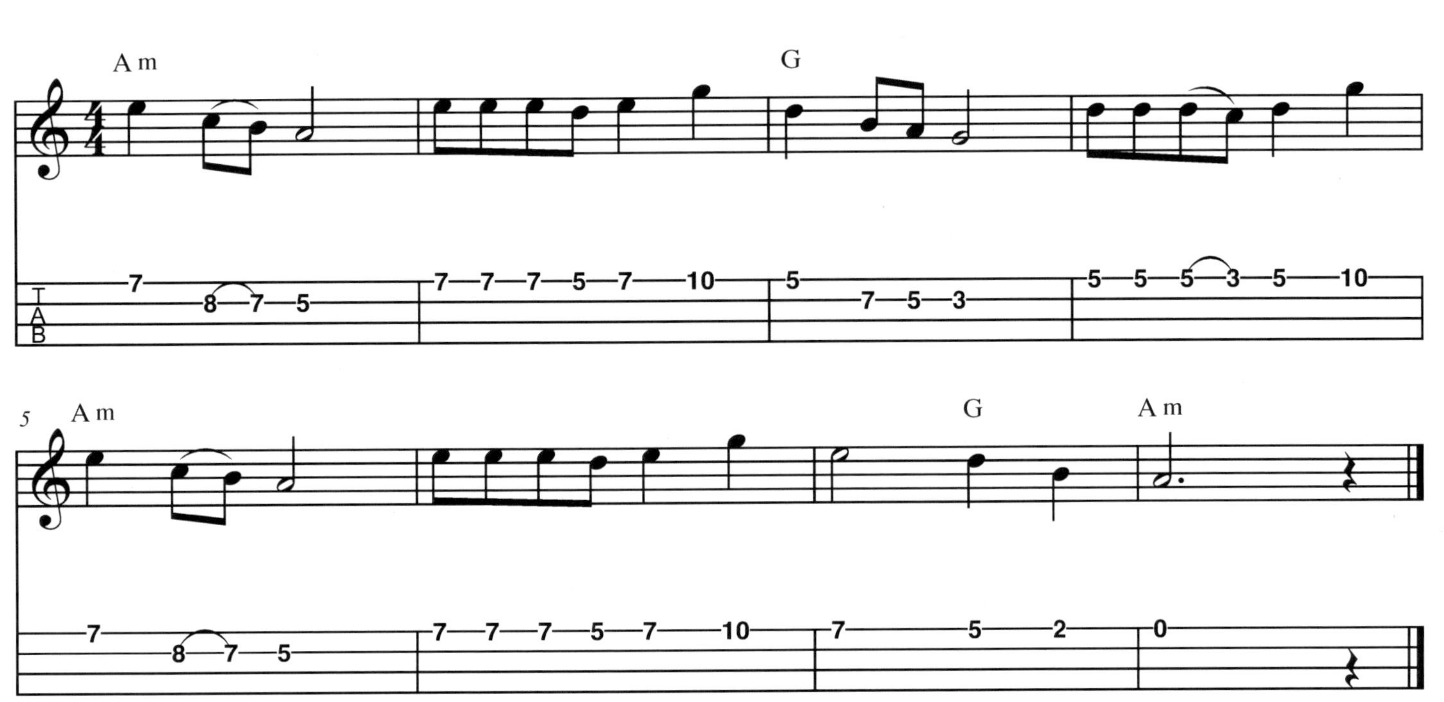

Old Dan Tucker

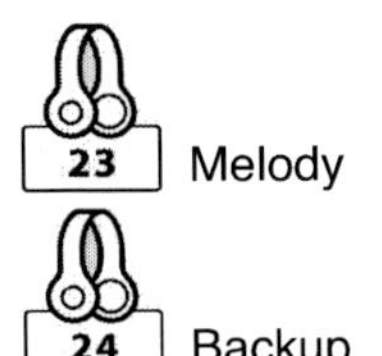

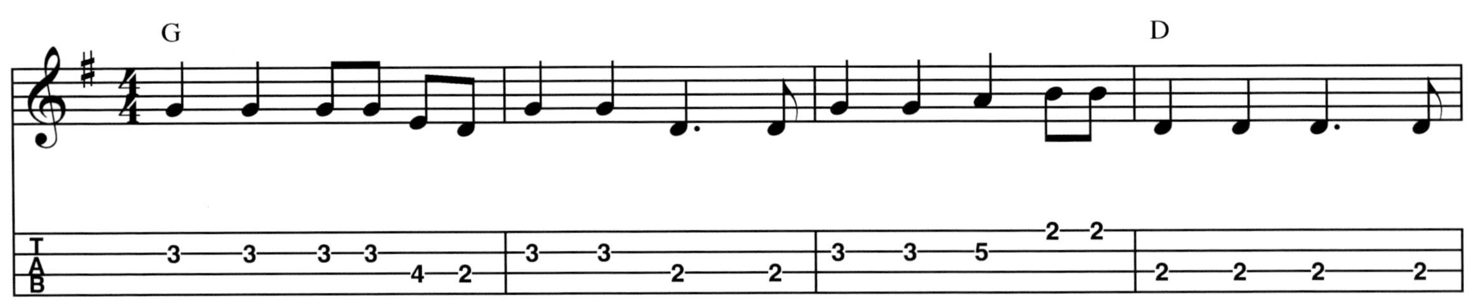

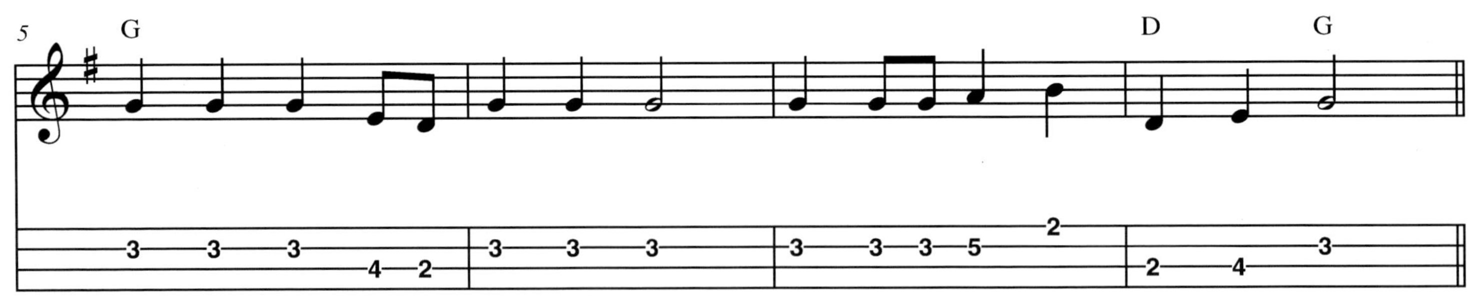

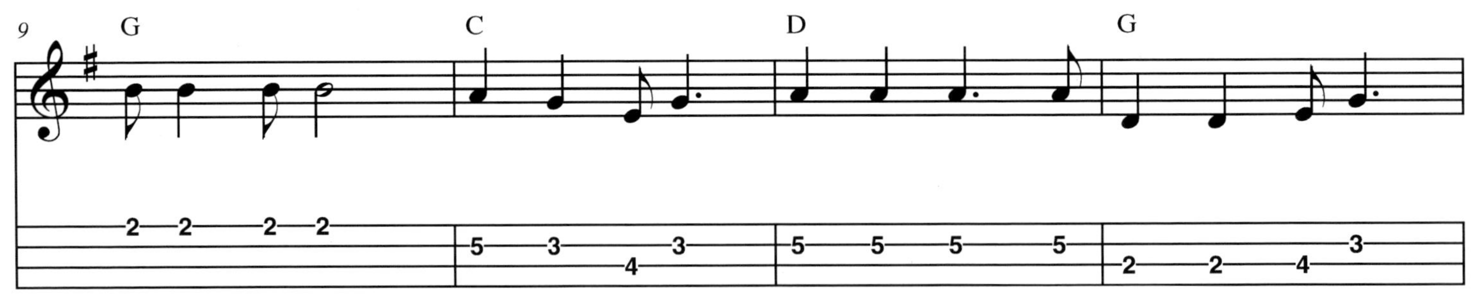

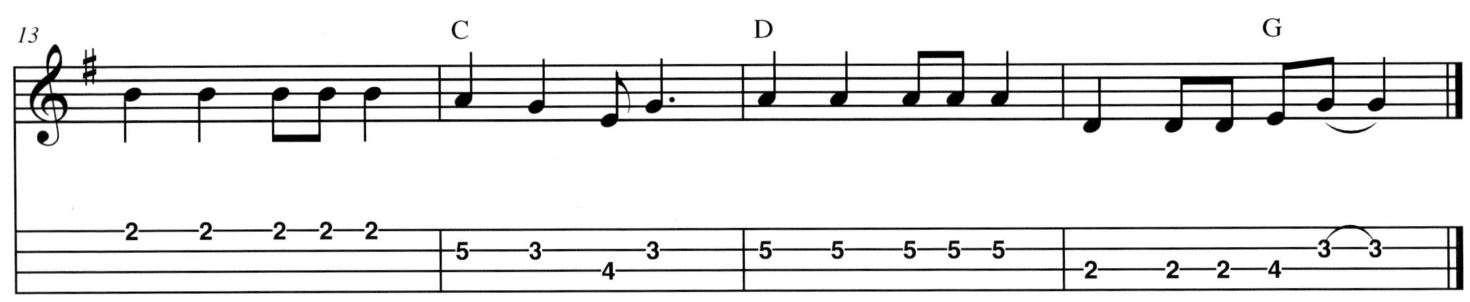

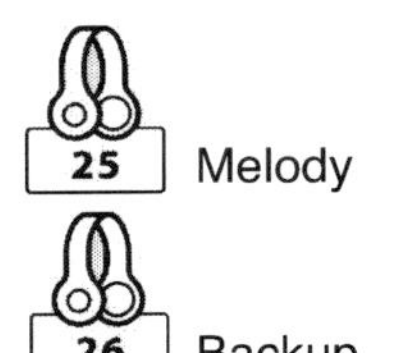

Old Joe Clark

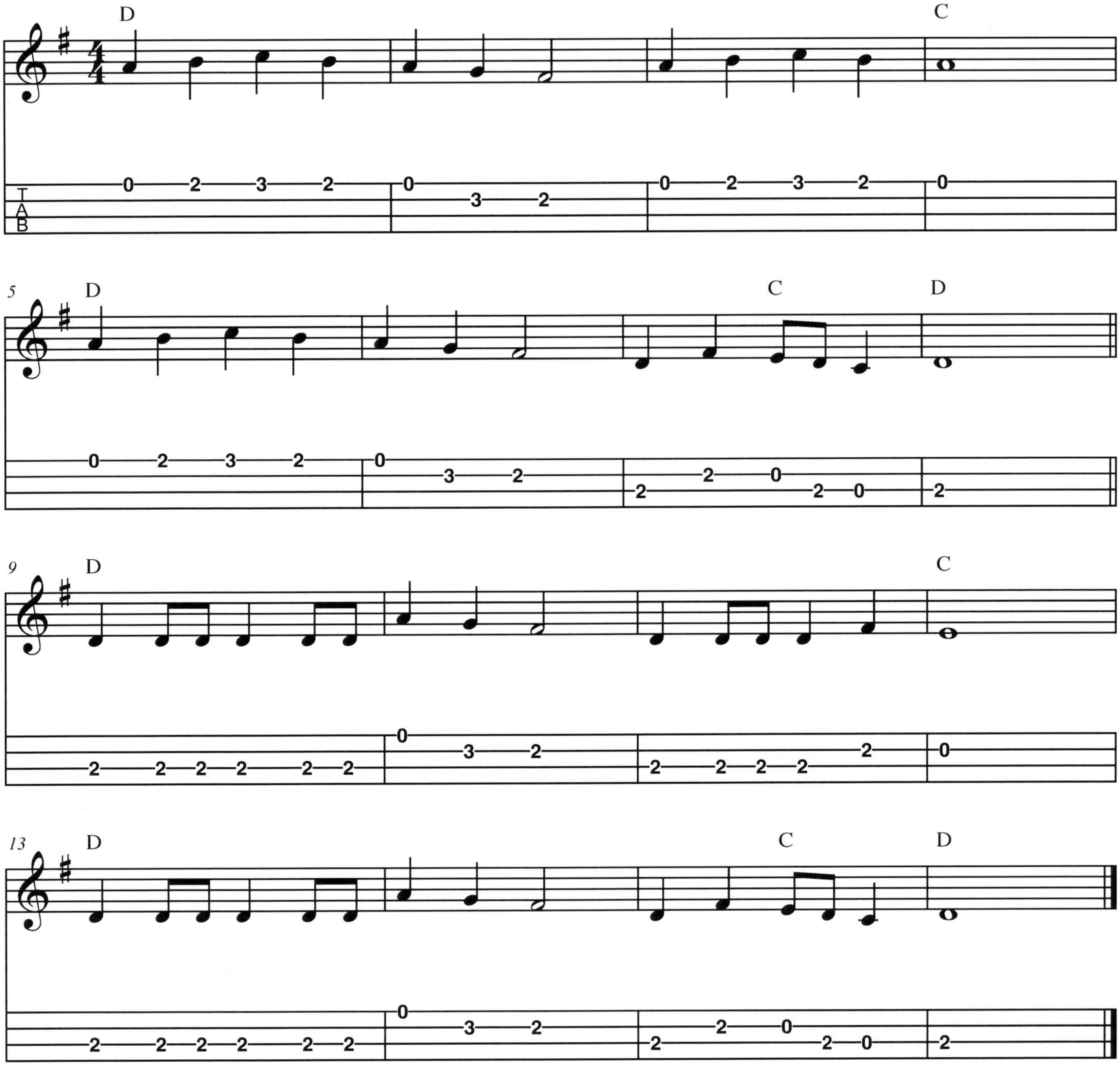

Planxty Irwin

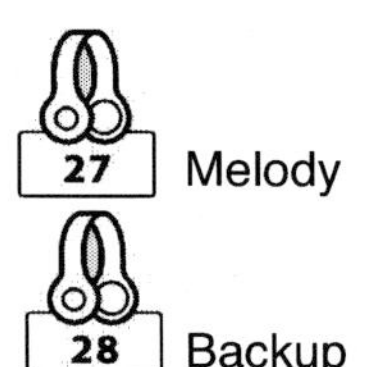

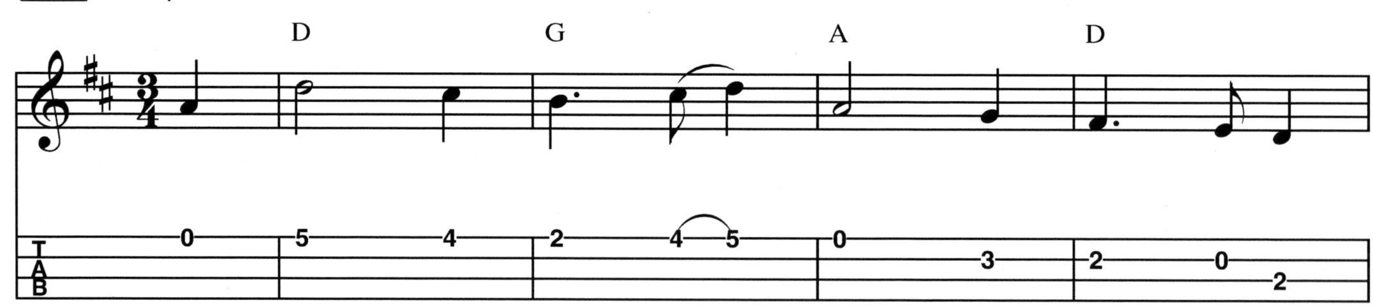

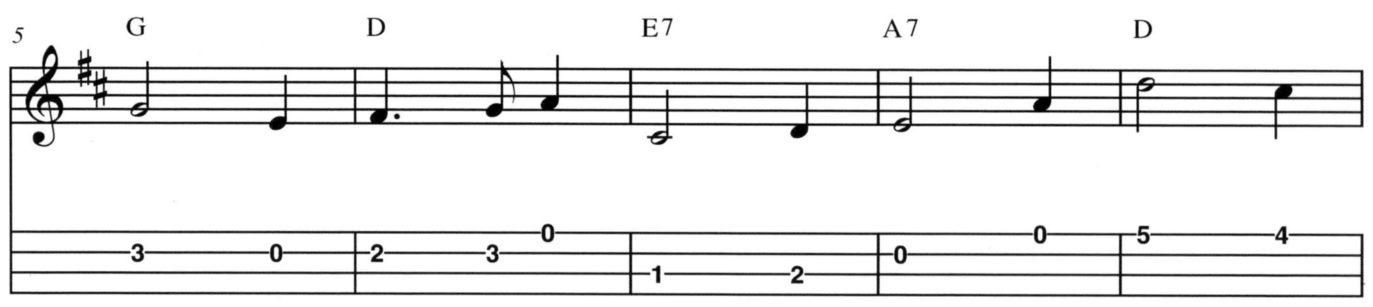

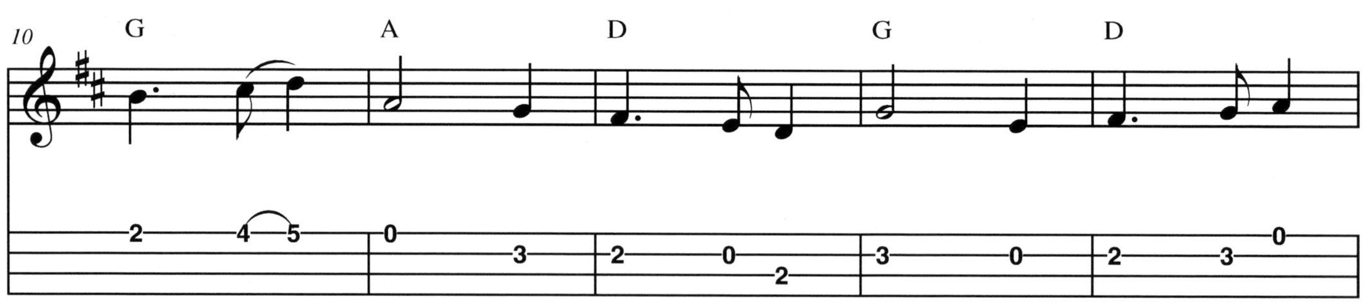

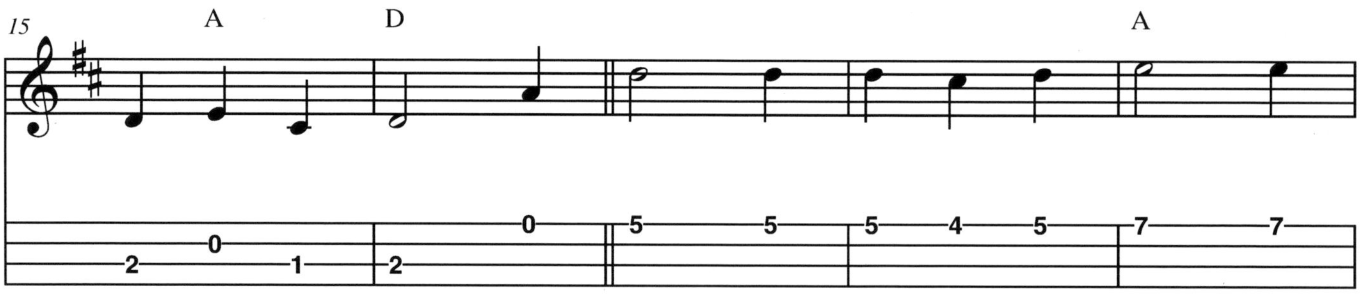

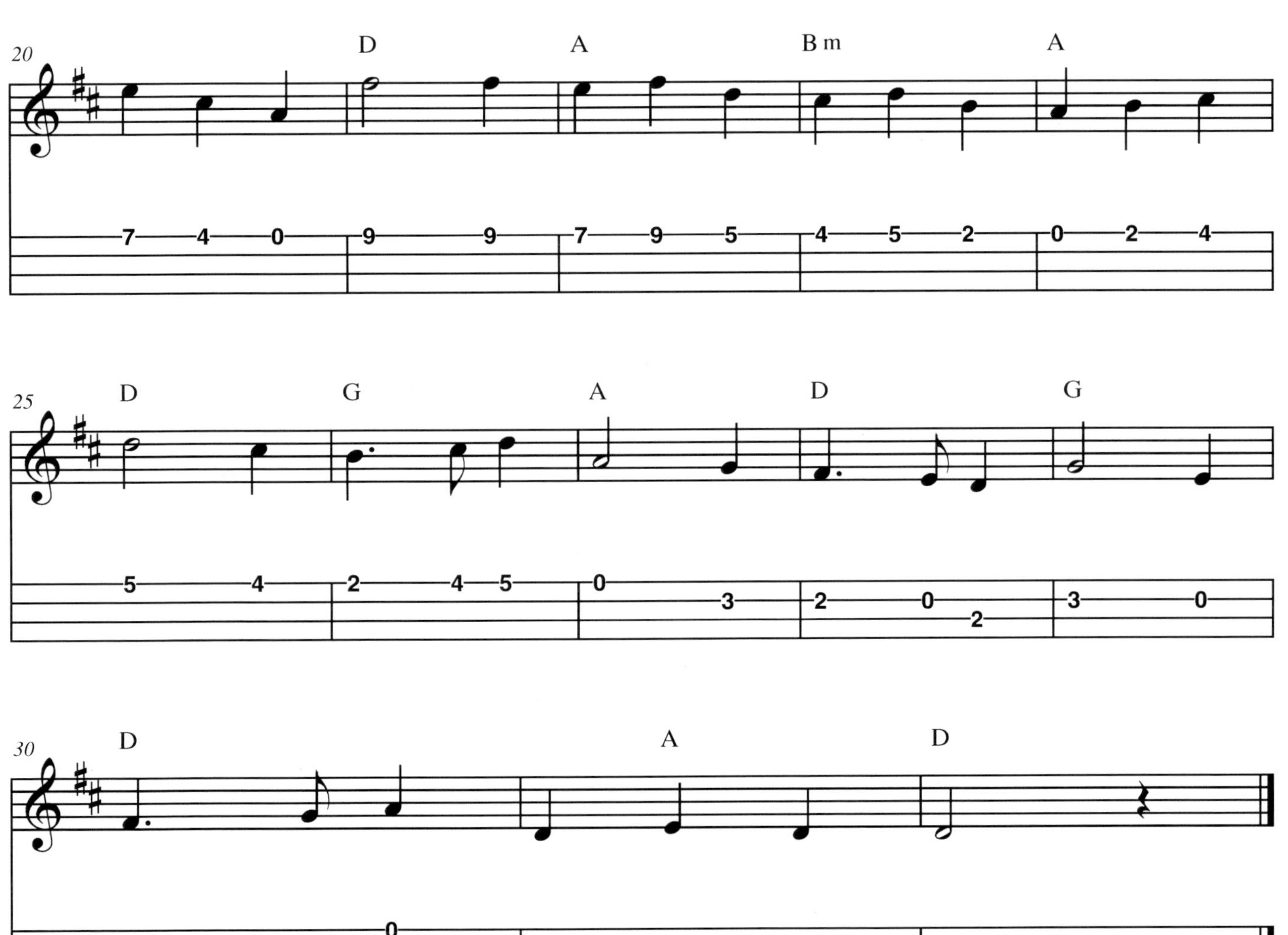
20
D
A
B m
A
25
D
G
A
D
G
30
D
A
D

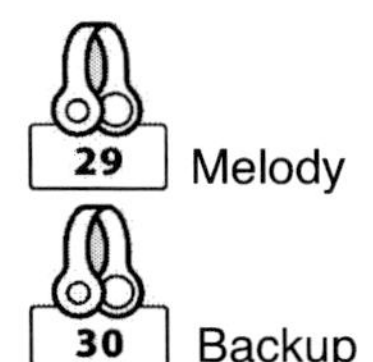

Roll in My Sweet Baby's Arms

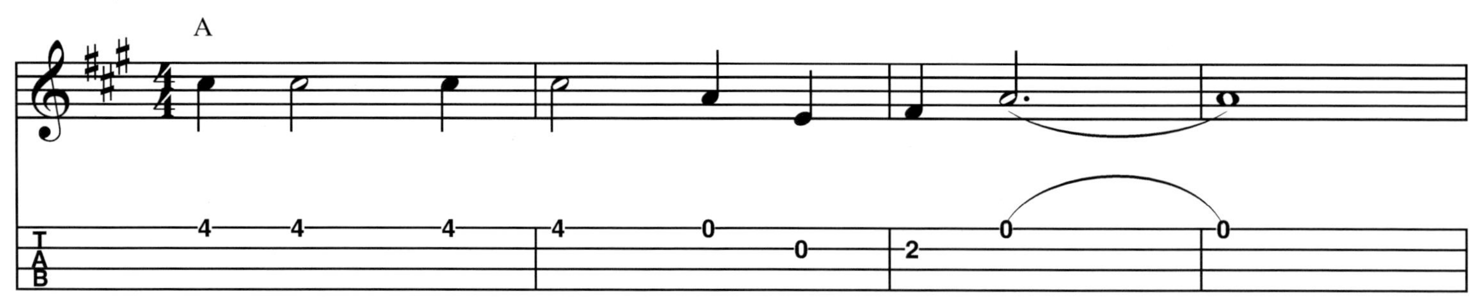

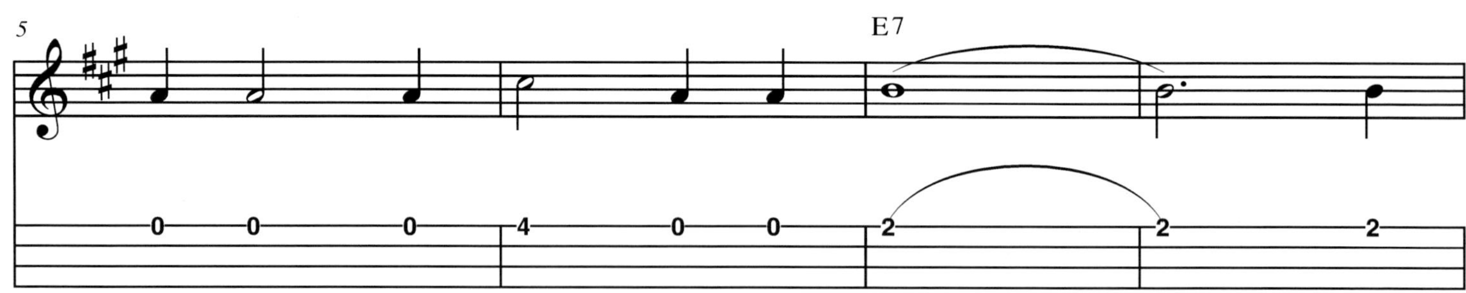

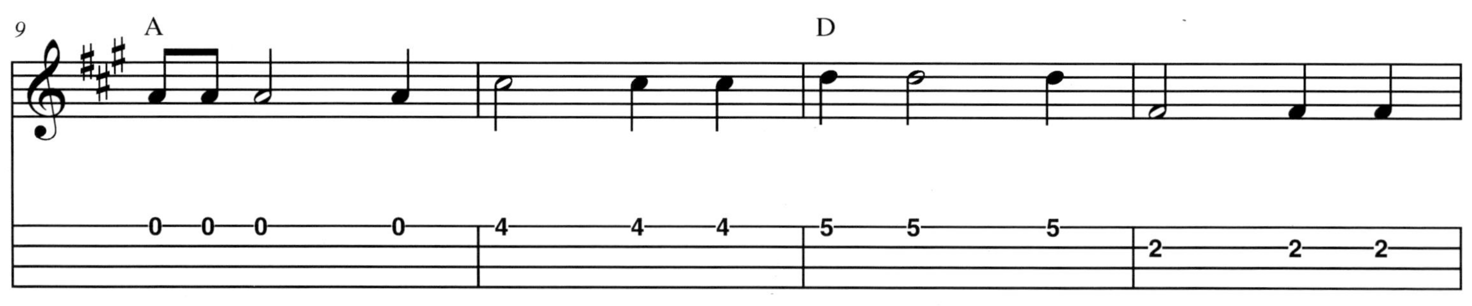

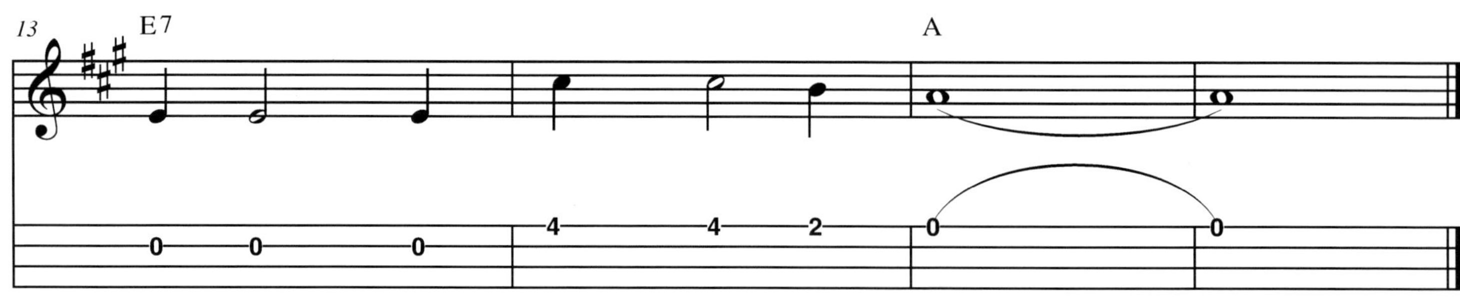

Shady Grove

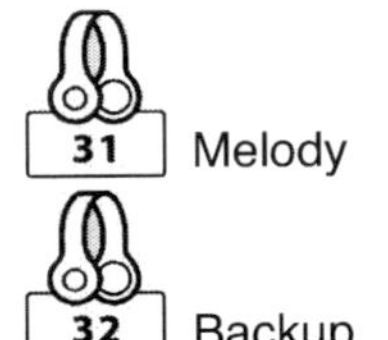

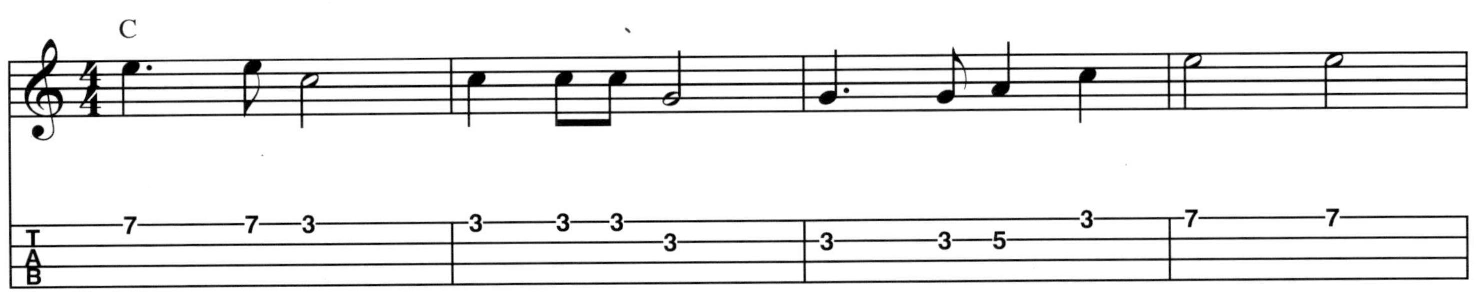

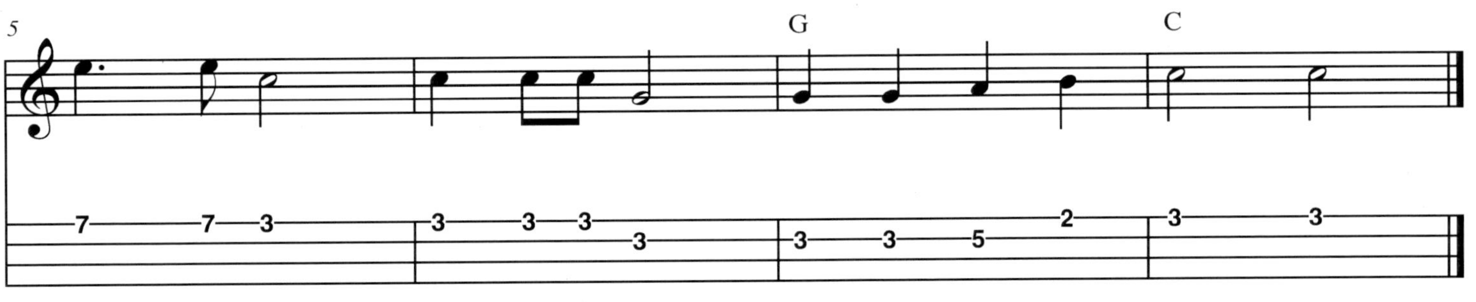

Sourwood Mountain

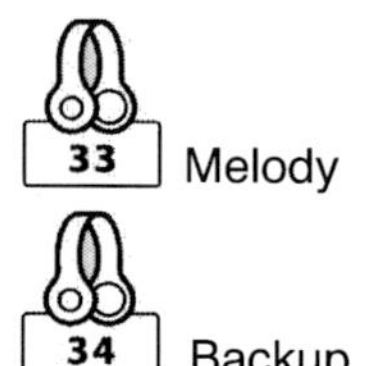

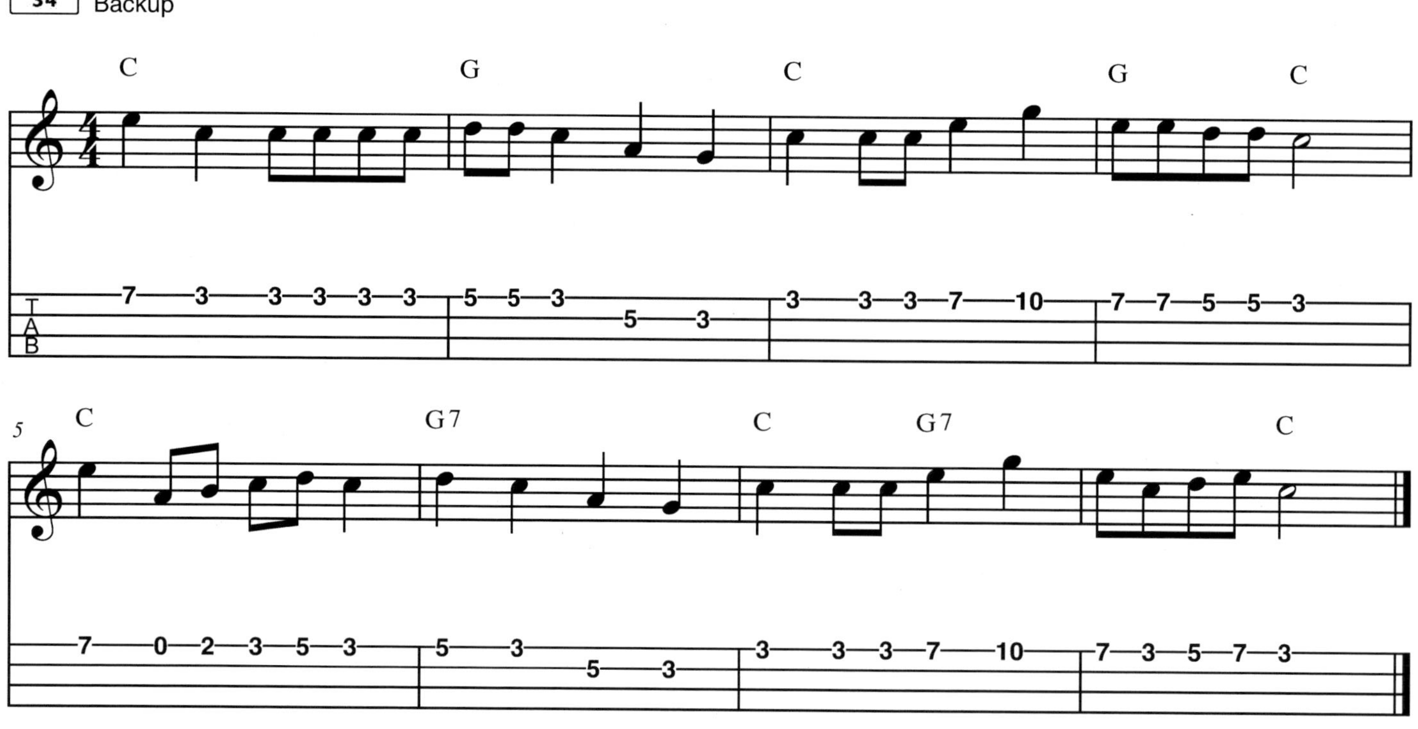

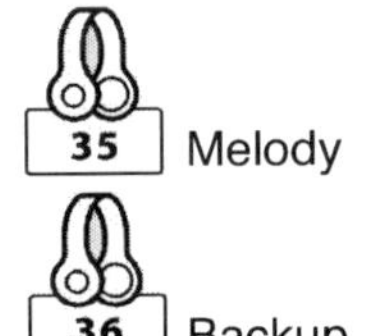

The Wabash Cannonball

G

3 C D7

6 1. G

9 2. G

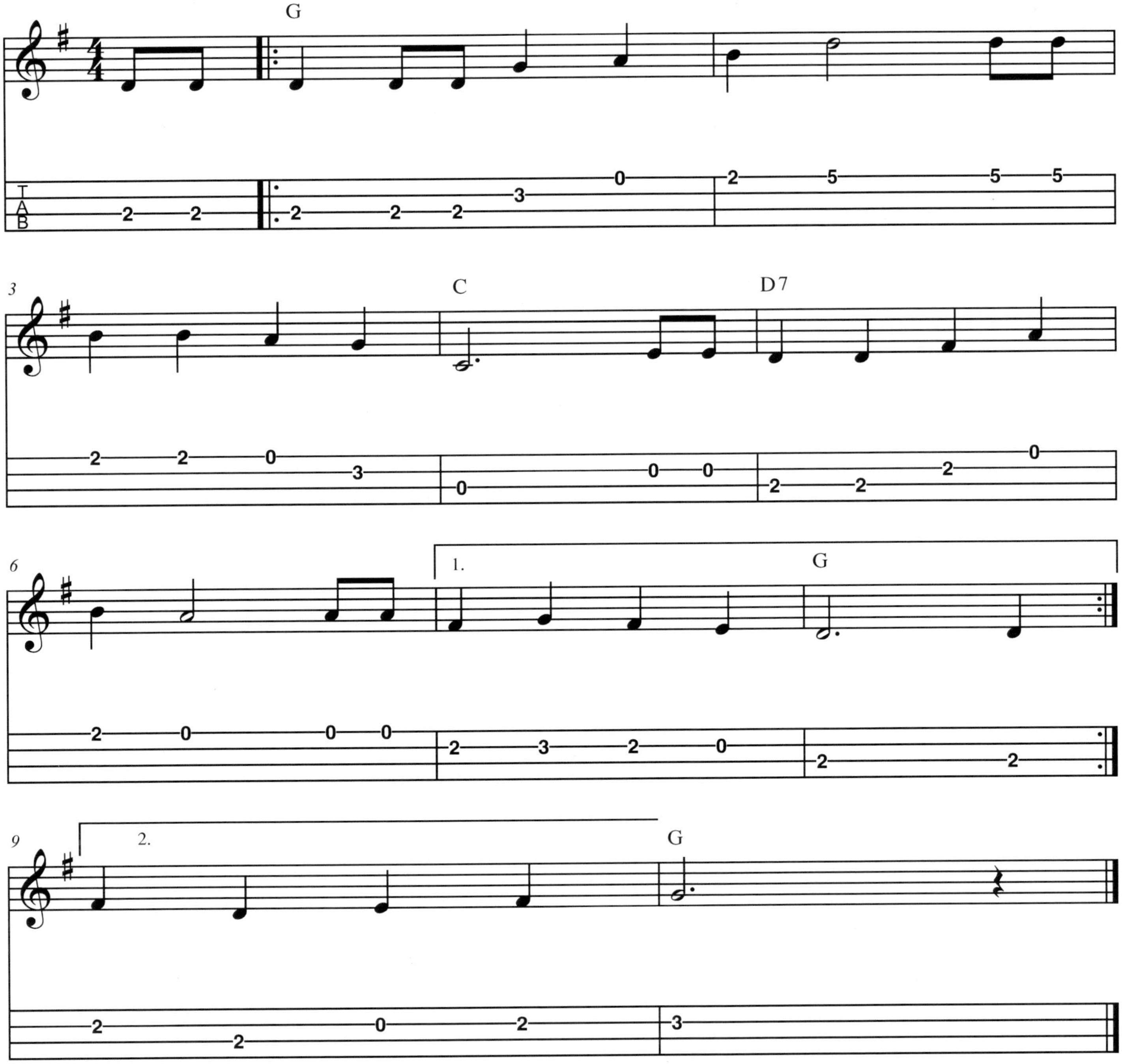

Wildwood Flower

37 Melody

38 Backup

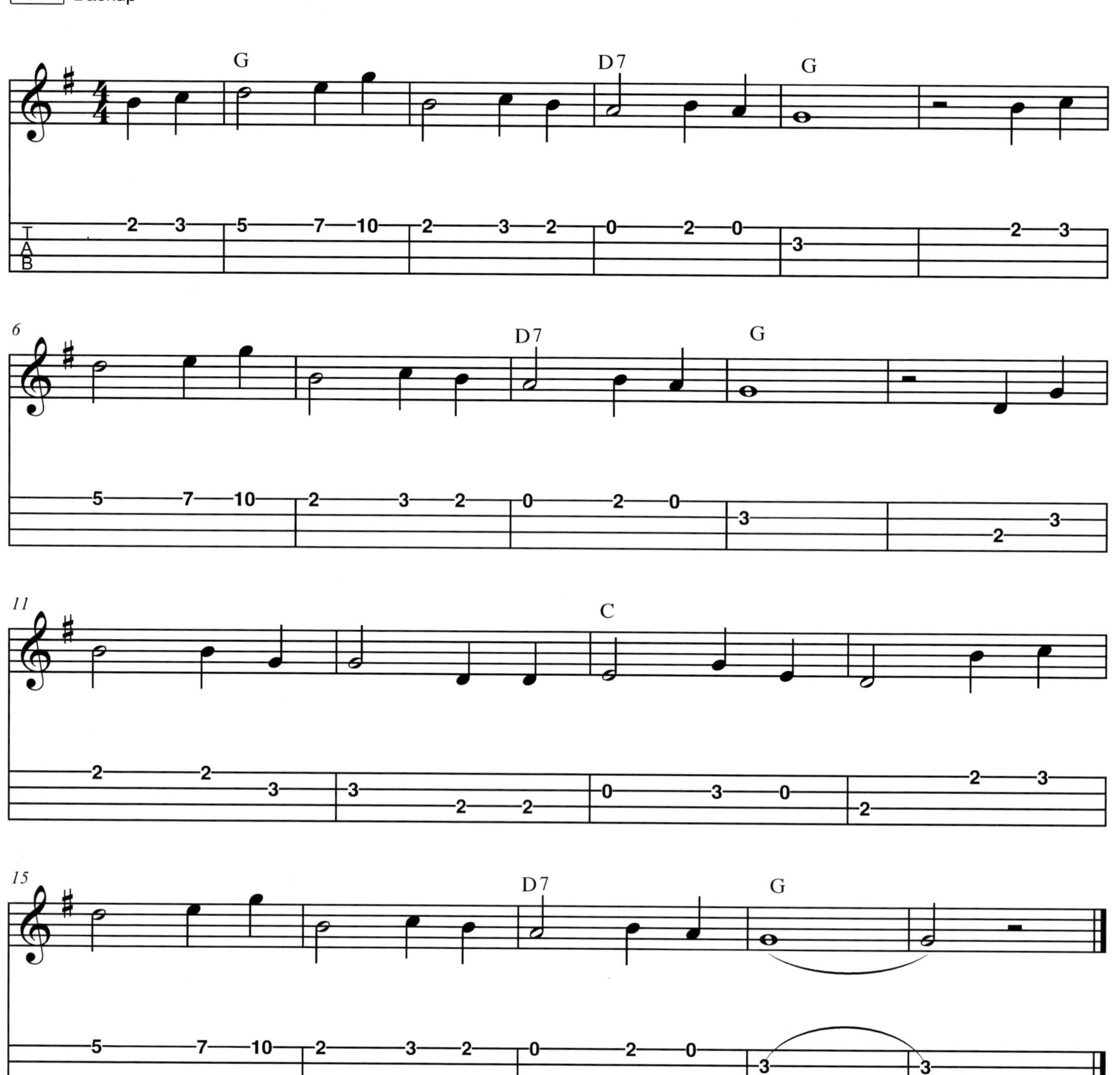

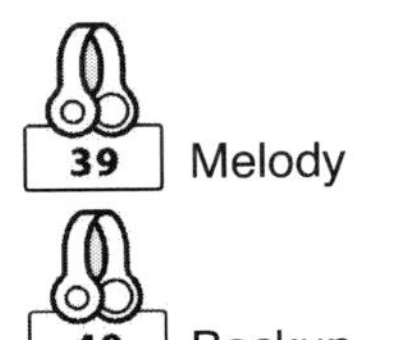

Will The Circle Be Unbroken

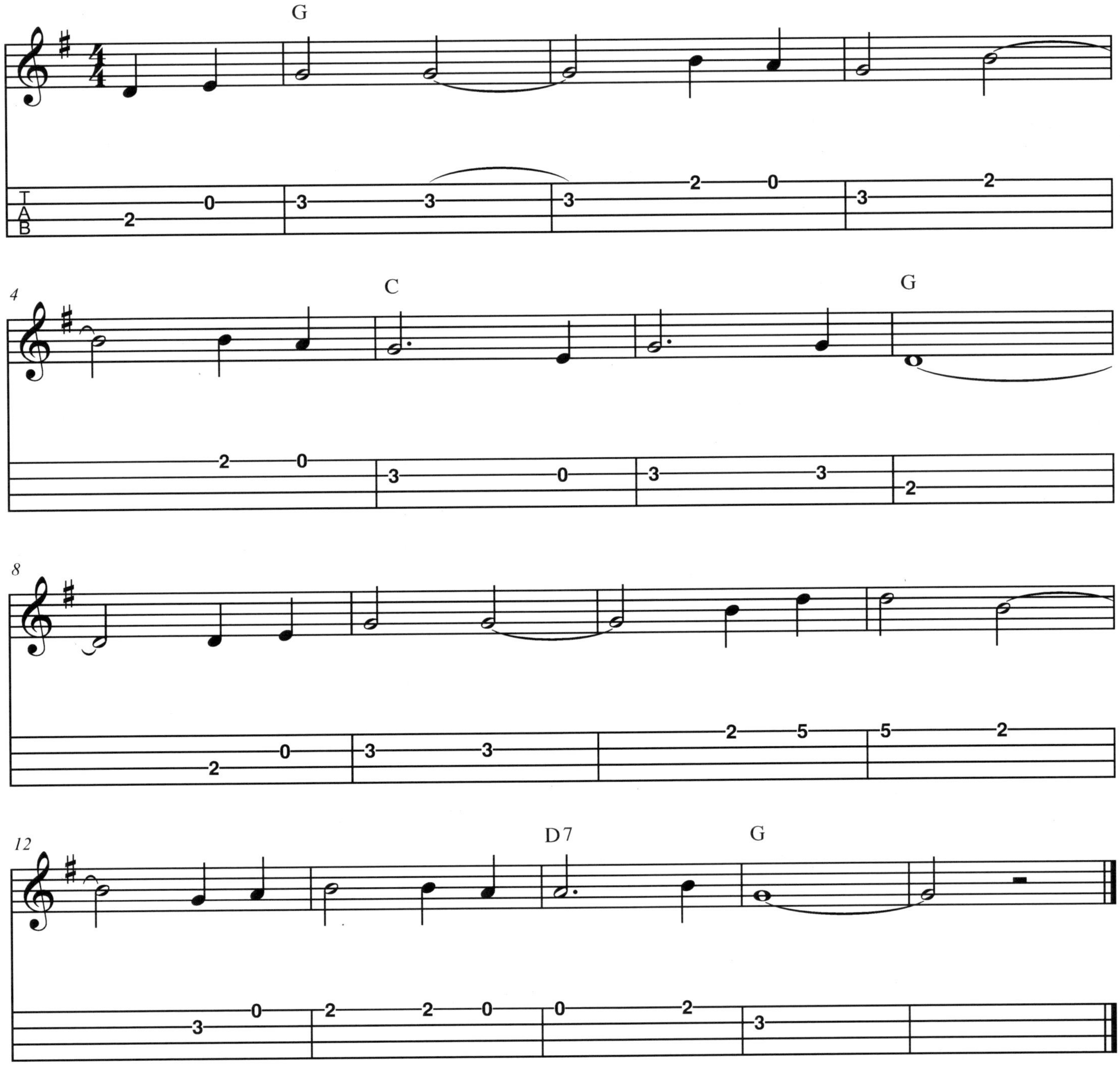

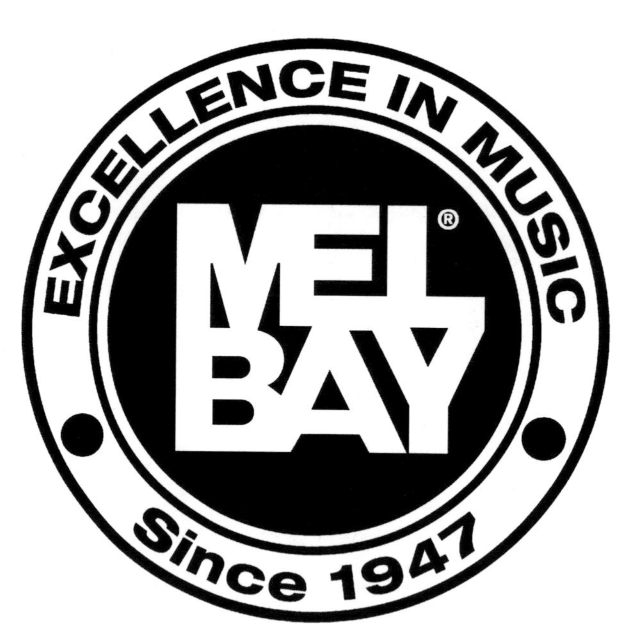

WWW.MELBAY.COM